Thanks for all of your help!

Presented to

Christine

From

Elizabeth Lake

Date

June 23, 2004

A CLASSROOM TEACHER COLLECTION

"WHAT TIME IS RECESS?"

Written and Compiled by Jeannie S. Williams

Cover Illustration: Sydney Tate Williams

Typography and Page Design: Donna McAfee

Summary: A collection of comments (serious, reverent, and humorous) young children have written about teachers.

ISBN 1-886648-00-X

Printed in the United States of America

CRAFTMASTERS BOOKS
P.O. Box 669
Sikeston, MO 63801-0669

"Pretty much all the
honest truth-telling
there is in the world,
is done by children . . ."
— *Oliver Wendell Holmes*

This book is dedicated to my
four year-old granddaughter, Tate.

Because one day very soon
she will ask "What Time Is Recess?"

And also to Tate's teachers,
Because one day very soon
they will exclaim —

"Lord, please don't let it rain at recess!"

THE IDEA FOR THIS BOOK came one day when I was invited to visit a first grade class during National Education Week. I talked to the children about the importance of learning to read and shared some of my favorite stories with them.

Mrs. Scott, the classroom teacher told her students one of the first things she did when she got home from work was sit down for a few moments and read. She told the children reading helped her relax. Suddenly the room became very quiet. No one said a word . . . finally a little boy in the back of the room slowly raised his hand and asked: "Where do you work, Mrs. Scott?"

While Mrs. Scott laughingly tried to explain that teaching was her work, I grabbed a pencil and quickly wrote down some of the comments the children offered.

The freedom of writing and drawing helps children and adults to stop, notice and appreciate the experience. This book is the result of listening to the children. As you explore the creativity of these budding writers and illustrators, you'll feel the need to encourage children to expand their positive abilities . . . the foundations are lasting.

— *Jeannie S. Williams*

1

A teacher can be anybody who is short or tall or skinny or fat. They can be black or white or they can be a man or a woman. Most of them that I know are short, fat white women . . .
— *Kyle, age 8*

A teacher is a good thing to have around the house.
My mom is one . . .
— *Katie, age 7*

A teacher is a very polite lady who always
uses a handkerchief to blow her nose . . .
— *Bryan, age 6*

If I could change school, I'd get rid
of all of them . . . — *Bruce, age 8*

Teachers will tell on you for anything and
you can't do a darn thing about it!
— *Lonnie, age 8*

A teacher is someone who always smells . . .
I mean always smells nice.
— *Rachel, age 7*

Most teachers are pretty old.
Like around 35 or 36 at least . . .
— *Britt, age 6*

I like my teacher, Mrs. Bates. She is pretty and nice.
I will tell you a secret. I will marry her when I grow up
if she is not already pregnant . . .   — *Calvin, age 7*

The most funniest thing that ever happened at school during
my whole life was when Mrs. Brown was getting some big
books off the top of the gray cabinet. (Mrs. Brown is not her
real name. Our teacher said we could change the name
in our stories to protect her privates . . .)

Well, she got up on a chair to get the books and we wondered
if she might fall because she is pretty fat. But she did
not fall. She just "tooted" real loud. (I hope you know what
that means!) She acted like she didn't "toot" but all of us
could smell it and we laughed so hard we almost died.
Well, we all got into trouble because we were laughing
so hard and she made us put our heads down on our desk.
Now you know the rest of the story . . .
— *Nathan, age 8*

Teachers will write your name on the board if you talk.
If you talk about three times you have to stand outside
until it gets real dark . . . and it don't even matter if
it is coming a storm, you still will have to stand there.
— *Benita, age 6*

A teacher is
a person with
a sad smile . . .
I think her shoes
must hurt her feet!
— *Becky, age 7*

5

Teachers do not live as long as regular people do. This is a true fact. I looked it up . . .
— *Ned, age 7*

6

The funniest thing I ever saw was when Mrs. Sanders came
to school with a potato chip stuck in her panty hose.
We saw it on the back of her leg and wondered how it got in there . . .
— *Nathan, age 8*

My dad told me this joke to tell my teacher. I did but she
didn't laugh. He said, "You can tell a teacher by the PUPILS
in her eyes . . ." I think it's pretty funny, don't you?
— *Matt, age 9*

Some teachers are normal and some are witches.
So far I've had 1 normal and 2 witches.
This is pretty scary when you think about it . . .
— *Joey, age 7*

My teacher is so nice. She will give you a hug everyday.
Some of the boys try to run away when she hugs them.
I told them they need to stand there and take it like a man!
— *Kara, age 7*

Being a teacher is a hard job. I am going to be one when
I grow up. The hardest part is keeping the kids in their seats
and making the bathroom smell good. The boys are the ones
who make the mess in there.   — *April, age 7*

When I was a kid, I liked school.
But the older I got the more I didn't like it.
— *David, age 8*

All of the teachers at our school were born before the War.
You can read more about it at your local public library . . .
— *Gloria, age 7*

Most teachers were born dirt poor. They should all play the lottery
and try to get rich quick if they want more money. But they
should remember — You can't win, if you don't play!
— *Blake, age 8*

Lots of teachers are real nice. Lots of them are not.
Some of them like kids. Some of them don't like kids.
None of them will hit kids. That is not their job.
It is the principal's job so stay away from him.
— *Jackie, age 6*

My favorite part of school is recess,
lunch and when the bell rings to go home.
— *Brandon, age 6*

Our principal does not have any hair on top of his head. He has some on the sides but he is a baldheaded man. I would like to rub his head if he would let me. It will bring you good luck to do that.
— *Terrell, age 8*

Everybody says my teacher looks just like a man named "Rush Limbo". I don't know if this is true or not because I never heard of the man, myself. Have you?
— *Stanley, age 8*

Teachers like to make up rules. They do it to try and keep peace and quiet at school. Sometimes it works and sometimes it don't!
— *William, age 7*

 I wish my teacher was my mom . . .
— *Libby, age 6*

The only way to fool a teacher is to learn how to whisper without moving your lips . . .   — *Brad, age 8*

You go to school to learn. So far I haven't learned much . . .
— *Hunter, age 7*

I don't want to go to school but my mom says I have to. I have 2 brothers and 1 sister who already went to school. Why can't they just teach me things?   Don't you think this would be a good idea? My mom says it won't work but I'd like to know what you think . . .
— *Skipper, age 7*

 Teachers need to learn how to keep their tempers down . . .
— *Liane, age 6*

A teacher can take the meanness right out of you when she wants to.
— *Blake, age 7*

A teacher doesn't make as much money as a married man . . . If they want to buy a new couch, they have to save up their money for a long, long time.
— *Larry, age 8*

If you have a baby and you are a teacher, the principal will take it out of your paycheck.
— *Barbara, age 7*

My dad is a teacher. My mom is a teacher. My Uncle Harlan is a principal. When I grow up I am going to be a priest like Father Bill because all of my family wants me to go to heaven when I die . . .
— *Scott, age 7*

The first thing you need to do if you want to be a teacher is grow up . . .
— *Alison, age 6*

If you have a good teacher, you always want to go to school . . .
— *Amber, age 8*

A teacher never has to go to the bathroom. She can sit there all day long and hold it.
— *Lauren, age 6*

We need to pray for our teachers.
Somebody took God out of
the school and won't let Him
help the teachers anymore.
I'm not real sure about this
but I think my dad said
the Democrats did it . . .
— *Steven, age 9*

14

My teacher is smart. She can count to ten backwards with her eyes closed.
— *Phillip, age 6*

My teacher got married the other day and now she has a new name. I think she regrets it.
— *Keith, age 8*

My teacher said it is OK if you mess up sometimes. She says everybody messes up sometimes. I wish she would tell my dad that.
— *Brandon, age 9*

Teachers give too much homework. It's a bad habit they have.
— *Leslie, age 8*

The hardest part about school is sitting in the chairs all day long. Your butt gets really sore and if you try to rub it the teacher will yell at you and say "Quit picking at your bottom!"
— *Jason, age 7*

We had another teacher yesterday, Mrs. Cannon was sick. Her name was Mrs. Wolf. She was as mean as her name. — *Barton, age 8*

G.R. and his big sister and his little sister had to go home and then the school nurse came in our room and looked in our hair. The teacher said we might have the headlights. — *Jay, age 6*

When I was in Kindergarten I took my grandma's teeth for Show and Tell. The teacher freaked out — — *Taylor, age 8*

Teachers are either men or women. None of them is ever neutral. — *Lance, age 8*

Everytime I draw a horse
on my paper Miss Dillard
says "that is a good dog that
you drawed." I guess she has
never seen a real horse . . .
— *Tina, age 7*

17

Heaven is full of good teachers
who have passed on . . .
— *Kimberly, age 8*

18

My teacher is named Mrs. Refering.   She came to our school
from another country. I will go there someday and visit her people.
I bet they are all nice. *[Mrs. Refering is from Mexico, Missouri]*
— *Crader, age 8*

Mrs. Robinson who teaches in the third grade is some kin to me.
Her mother is kin to my mother's brother-in-law's family by marriage
from Zelma. I think we are first cousins on her side of the family.
— *Jaynell, age 9*

Some teachers have secret lives.
I saw one at the grocery store wearing SHORTS!
— *Chris, age 8*

I am trying real hard to be good at school. My dad said if I get a
spanking at school I will get another one when I get home.
I'm really praying this don't happen during my lifetime . . .
— *Derek, age 7*

My teacher is very nice. I enjoy watching her perform.
— *Mike, age 9*

Five of the kids in our room are sick.
The teacher said they all have the chicken cops.
— *Brenna, age 7*

My teacher read us a story about an old lady who swallowed a fly.
Where does she get this stuff? — *Myron, age 7*

Our teacher is really worried about the boys
in our room. They don't have good manners and
they forget to zip up their pants . . .
— *Cari, age 7*

At Halloween our teacher dressed up like a real pretty woman.
She never looked so good in all of her entire life.
— *Blake, age 7*

My teacher is pretty.
She fluffs up her hair a lot.
— *Anna, age 6*

Mrs. Taylor was my first grade teacher I liked her best.
She is still pretty but you can tell she is aging fast.
— *Amanda, age 9*

One word that describes my teacher is strict. Two words that describe my teacher is strict and skinny. Three words that describe my teacher is strict, skinny and religious. She is a nun.
— Thomas, age 9

My teacher said we are going to get a real
[Christmas] tree for our room. We will put it
in the corner by the big book shelf.
I wonder where we will put the Baby Jesus?
— *Misty, age 8*

I Like To Go To School
by Megan, age 7

I like to go to school. I like to count.
I like to read. I like to paint.
I like recess. I like to swing.
I play with Jenny.

Everyday we say, "What time is recess?"
And the teacher says —
"If you ask me that again, I will scream!"

So far she does not scream.
But this is just the start of school and
I think she is still trying to be nice . . .

THE END.

24

IN CONCLUSION, I hope this is not THE END . . . When I decided to go directly to the voices of the children and let them speak in this book, I had almost forgotten how the thoughts of children delight us grown-ups. We are so delighted because of the vast gulf between their world and ours. Where we adults see the tired old classroom of everyday life, children see a new world waiting to be explored. They are wiser than we are in a way, because we have forgotten the magic of things . . .

I would love to read any "teacher" stories and comments that come from your classroom. Send them to me and together you and I will listen to the voices of the children and perhaps we can "let the magic begin" the next time a child in our classroom asks — "What Time Is Recess?"

Jeannie S. Williams
201 Nancy Drive
Sikeston, MO 63801

25

P.S.

My teacher is a very great lady. I want to be just like her when I grow ~~up~~ up.

She really touches my heart.

Jessica

94 95 96 97 98 99 00 01 12 11 10 9 8 7 6 5 4 3 2